The

Will Edwards

PAPERBACK EDITION

First Published: 2006

Paperback: Dec 2018

This Revision: Feb 2019

For Fay, with love from me and the starfish.

This book is provided for own your personal use. No portion of this book may be reproduced in any form except as permitted by U.S. copyright law. You may not change this book or distribute it without the prior written permission of the publisher.

Copyright © White Dove Books 2006 – 2019

Contents

WHAT PEOPLE ARE SAYING	3
INTRODUCTION	5
YOUR WAKE-UP CALL	7
COMMITMENT	9
AN OPEN MIND	12
PERSISTENCE	15
FLEXIBILITY	20
FAITH	23
THANKFULNESS	27
PASSION	33
THERE IS NO FAILURE	36
THE JOURNEY TO SUCCESS	45
SPIRITUAL PRINCIPLES	49
UNIVERSAL PRINCIPLES	53
THE REST OF YOUR LIFE	56
CHANGING THE WORLD	61
MORE BY WILL EDWARDS	64
APPENDIX A: GRATITUDE JOURNAL	65
APPENDIX B: SUCCESS QUOTES	76
THE BACK STORY	78

What People Are Saying

With grateful thanks to the following people who left encouraging comments at my website.

"I really enjoyed reading this book. I believe it will change my life and I thank the author for writing such a wonderful book." - Muhammad Shakir

"Very helpful book, really made a great impact on me. Thank you." - Silard Matrai

"It really changed my life so I want to tell others about this book. Thanks." - Andnet Wolde

"This book has the capacity to transform people." - Daniel

"God bless you - a sentence in the book changed my life." - Joseph Nii Kwtia Hammond

"This is a life changing and interesting book and I liked it very much!" - Workineh

"Thanks! Your book changed my life." - Benedette

"Thanks and God bless you for doing a great work to change the lives of many people." – Lawrence

Thank you to everyone who left such wonderful comments on *Google Play*, including the following people.

"So inspiring. I loved every detail of your writing, inspiring me with its every word." - Niyukti Jain

"Extremely helpful. I enjoyed every minute of this book. I've been applying these attributes to my everyday life an there's definitely been a change." - Yung Spadez

"It's a wonderful mind-opening book, awesome. Love it." - Naorem Langlen

"Unbelievable! It truly felt as if it was written just for me, especially at such a difficult and depressing phase of my life." - Nikil Khatri

"This is a great inspiration to me. Thank you. God bless you!" - Ayanah Battle

"I was totally captivated from the minute I started reading this book. Exactly what I needed and will definitely be applying these seven keys in my life." - Jacquelene Chapman

Introduction

"Success means having the courage, the determination, and the will to become the person you believe you were meant to be." - George Sheehan

Many texts on the subject of success begin by offering a definition of the term or by encouraging the reader to think about what success might mean to the individual. There is nothing wrong with that, at all. It is naturally a good idea to properly define a goal before beginning to work towards achieving it.

However, real satisfaction comes not from achieving goals for their own sake, but by making a contribution to society as a whole; by finding the one thing that really gets you excited, engages your talents and rewards you financially. Something that is truly worthy of your time and energy, that you enjoy doing; something you can take pride in doing, that makes you feel good. We believe that not only does such a thing exist, it is actually the reason you were born: to find and fulfil your *life-purpose*.

A difficulty for many people is that they do not see themselves as anything particularly special, and they do not believe that life holds any real meaning. They are in very good company; many successful people, at least initially, thought exactly the same thing. But somewhere along the line, they were challenged to think differently about themselves and their lives.

The purpose of this book is to challenge your thinking about who you are and why you are here and my hope, in writing, is that you will begin to see yourself as a special person, with a truly unique purpose in life - because that is the truth!

Your Wake-Up Call

When I was quite young, someone told me, "If you want to be really successful, find out what God wants you to do with your life and then dedicate yourself to achieving it".

At the time, I didn't really like that idea; I did not believe that my life could have any particular purpose and I did not think that anything God might have in mind would be of any interest to me in any case. Gradually, I have come to believe that what that person said to me, all those years ago, is true.

As human beings, we all share certain basic wants and needs: we have need for food, water, shelter, safety, love, respect and self-esteem. We all share an in-built tendency, as Freud stated, to want to move away from pain and toward pleasure. This tendency is part of the human condition for our own good; it keeps us away from harm and generally helps us to make good choices.

Most people settle for pursuing a career that satisfies these basic human wants and needs and never really think beyond them to what their life *could* be about. Somewhere along the line, I came to realise that what God wanted for me, and what I wanted, were one and the same thing. This understanding came after I had determined to find out what God actually wanted me to do with my life.

It was a profound moment for me. I gradually came to understand my inner hopes, dreams and deepest desires as being implanted by God. So pursuing God's purpose for my life was, in fact, also pursuing my own true purpose. When it really came down to it, I finally realised that I needed to look within to discover my own purpose and once I had found out what it was, it then became possible to dedicate myself to fulfilling it.

So my message to you is simple: it is time for you to wake-up! It is time for you to start thinking of your life in a different way. It is time for you to fulfil your dream - whatever that may be. That is why you are here on the planet right now. By finding and fulfilling your own unique purpose in life you will be living your life to the full.

In this book, you will discover practical, tested principles that will bring success to you if you diligently apply them to your life. As you will see, they are unerring, timeless, universal principles that always bring success to those who use them.

Commitment

Committedness: the trait of sincere and steadfast fixity of purpose.

Commitment: the act of binding yourself, intellectually or emotionally, to a definite course of action.

1. Commitment
2. An Open Mind
3. Persistence
4. Flexibility
5. Faith
6. Thankfulness
7. Passion

What are you doing with your Life? Would you say that you are living your dream or are you living from hand to mouth, making the best of things; just getting to the next week; what we might call existing, rather than living?

If you *are* living your dream, then well done: you are truly on the road to success. If you are not living your dream - or even if you have no dream at present - then do not despair because this little book was written for you. We are going to help you to find your dream, develop it and then to actually achieve it!

To live a truly successful life, you do need to first have a dream. As Carl Sandburg, American historian, poet and novelist put it, "nothing happens unless first a dream."

If you think about it, nothing at all now exists within our experience of physical reality that did not first exist in the mind of the person who made it or brought it into being. In all cases, everything is created twice: as Stephen Covey once put it, the physical creation follows the mental creation.

To succeed, you must have a dream, or you may prefer to call it a vision, and you must completely commit yourself to its ultimate fulfilment - that is the essence of the mental creation.

Here is one of the real secrets of success: you should dream big dreams because you can have anything you want! Read that statement again and let it really sink in because it is true that you can have anything you want; you can be anything you want to be and you can do anything you want to do. This may at first seem a bit self-indulgent to you, but your deepest desires constitute a strong indicator of your own life purpose.

What does it mean: to commit yourself to your dream? To illustrate, let me tell you a little about the story of Charles Lindbergh. You know, of course who he was - he was the first person to fly the Atlantic solo - non-stop all the way to Paris. An incredible feat which he eventually accomplished in May 1927.

He used to dream of flying across the Atlantic during his long haul flights delivering mail. Once he had imagined the possibility of being the first person to do this, he completely committed himself to its achievement overcoming all kinds of set-backs. He did not allow the negative opinions of the doubters who surrounded him to influence his resolve.

When he was unable to purchase the single aircraft in existence that he calculated would be capable of making that momentous journey, he had his own airplane designed and built. He didn't have the money, but he got a group of St Louis businessmen to sponsor him - that's why the plane was called *The Spirit of St Louis* - now that's commitment.

Once you have your dream, you too need to demonstrate that kind of resolve - and let me tell you plainly - you are capable of it!

It requires you to take actions that are congruent with your wishes in order to translate them into reality, but the first step is to have that dream - your own dream, not anyone else's ideas about what is best for you in life - and then absolutely commit yourself to its achievement.

An Open Mind

Openness: characterized by an attitude of ready accessibility about one's actions or purposes

Receptiveness: willingness or readiness to receive - especially impressions or ideas

1. Commitment
2. An Open Mind
3. Persistence
4. Flexibility
5. Faith
6. Thankfulness
7. Passion

Once you have committed yourself to achieving your dream, you should begin to notice something rather odd starting to happen in your life: the universe actually begins to help you to achieve it.

You just need to be open-minded - that is, you need to be ready and willing to receive what the universe (you might prefer to say God) has in store for you. Some people call this principle the *Law of Attraction*, but whatever you call it, it is quite true that you will absolutely set in motion unseen forces which will definitely assist you with the manifestation of your dream.

People, events and circumstances will be drawn to you that will actually assist you in the achievement of your dream. You can probably only fully accept this truth when you experience it for yourself and once you

have committed to your dream, you w[ill]
experience it. Things will start to hap[pen. They may]
seem like co-incidence at first, but yo[u are experiencing]
an altered reality.

As an example of this principle i[n action, let's take a]
brief look at the true story of Rudy Ruettiger. You may
know that Rudy had a dream. His dream - now the
subject of a truly inspiring movie - was to play football
(American) for Notre Dame. Everyone told him it
couldn't be done. But this is how the universe helped him
to achieve his dream.

When he was 22 years old, a friend bought him a
Notre Dame jacket for his birthday. When he presented it
to Rudy, he commented, 'Rudy, you were born to wear
this jacket!' These words somehow touched his heart and
he resolved, there and then, to do something about it. So
he took a bus en route to South Bend, Indiana, with the
specific goal of meeting the Notre Dame Championship
football coach, Ara Parseghian, to discuss the matter
further.

It turned out that Rudy needed to improve his grades
prior to ever being considered for Notre Dame, which he
did by attending Holly Cross Junior College. With
nowhere to live, he slept in the maintenance room and
after numerous applications and trials, Rudy was finally
accepted by Notre Dame and eventually made the
football team as a walk-on.

Rudy was not really considered good enough to play
for the team, but he never missed a practice match and
was there, suited-up during the final game of his senior

Now, many people in the crowd knew of Rudy's to play for the team and in the final minutes of the last game, the crowd started chanting: *Ru-dy! Ru-dy! Ru-dy!* Coach Dan Devine was so moved that he put him into the game in the last 27 seconds and, in the final play, he sacked the quarterback. Rudy was then carried off the field in triumph, on the shoulders of his teammates.

When you carry your own dream within, you too will be able to touch the hearts and minds of the people around you in much the same way and it is a truly wonderful and uplifting experience when you find out for yourself that the universe does indeed help you to achieve your goal.

Persistence

Persistence: refusing to give up, especially when faced with opposition or difficulty; continuing firmly or steadily

Persistence: the act of continually pursuing something in spite of obstacles

1. Commitment
2. An Open Mind
3. Persistence
4. Flexibility
5. Faith
6. Thankfulness
7. Passion

If having a dream and committing to its ultimate achievement is something like plotting your final destination ahead of an exciting journey, then persistence is rather like the engine you need in order to get there. Persistence is what drives you on to take the next step in your journey; persistence is what prevents you from getting discouraged by what may have happened in the past; persistence is where the rubber meets the road!

In his book *Touching the Void*, Joe Simpson recounts how he and his friend Simon Yates, climbed Siula Grande in the Peruvian Andes. The west face of this peak represented a major climbing challenge and it had never been climbed previously. They set out to climb it, alpine style, which, according to Joe, is the purest style of mountain climbing. It essentially consists of taking everything you need in your rucksack and climbing, with your partner, without any additional support of any kind.

After a strenuous and challenging ascent, they both made it to the summit and after a brief period of enjoying the moment, drinking in the feeling of exhilaration, they began their descent. It was whilst traversing the north ridge that Joe slipped and fell, breaking his leg badly. The impact drove his tibia through his kneecap and beyond his femur making it completely impossible for him to use his leg. Faced with this difficult situation, they hatched a plan to get Joe down the mountain, lowering him, by hand, using two 150 feet ropes tied together.

Simon would lower Joe 300 feet down the mountain. Joe would then stand on his good leg and take up the slack. Simon would then climb down to him and then they repeated the procedure. The matter was complicated slightly by the knot they had used to tie the two ropes together, since it would not pass through the apparatus they were using. They invented a signalling system to deal with this difficulty, and were making progress using the method when the weather, which had been very bad, got even worse.

In blizzard conditions, with night approaching, Simon inadvertently lowered Joe over an overhang. Unable to communicate because of the blizzard, Simon had no idea what had happened and hung on to the rope, gradually getting weaker and struggling with his footing. At the other end of the rope, Joe was dangling above a precipice with no ability to do anything. He tried to climb the rope, but because of frost bite, he dropped the equipment he needed to make the ascent.

After about hour and a half Simon made the agonising decision to cut the rope, racked with guilt because he felt it would mean certain death for his partner. He then dug a snow cave, spent the night on the mountain and made his descent the following day. Meanwhile, Joe miraculously survived the fall; he landed on a ledge inside a crevasse. Unable to climb out because of his broken leg, he lowered himself deeper into the crevasse.

Eventually he saw a shaft of light and he managed to crawl out. Then, after that strenuous climb and difficult descent with a badly fractured leg, having survived the 100 feet fall, stumbling again and again, in constant agony, he eventually hopped and crawled the remaining five miles all the way back down the mountain. He finally arrived at the camp, exhausted and delirious - it took him three days.

Like Joe's goal of getting himself down the mountain and back to safety, the goals we sometimes set for ourselves may seem completely overwhelming at times. But we can overcome the difficulties by using the same methods he employed. Faced with overwhelming odds and a truly gigantic goal, he continually broke the task into smaller goals, each of which he believed represented an achievable challenge.

He would challenge himself to crawl to a particular rock within twenty minutes. When he got there, he set himself another similar goal, and then another, and another. This was how he managed to mentally deal with the seemingly insurmountable task of getting himself back to camp. Of course, it might be argued that, in Joe's case, he had no other choice but, actually, he did. The other option would have been to simply give up. When you consider the sheer agony at every jar of his broken leg, on top of the exhausting climb, the second almost fatal fall and then the long journey, hauling his body in freezing conditions without food or water, it might have a lot been easier to give up, in many respects.

In your journey to success, you too will need to be resilient and persistent, especially at those times when everything might seem hopeless. You need to learn how to access that inner strength that you definitely possess, that makes you stronger than you think. Always remember that, as Pooh says in the Disney movie *Pooh's Grand Adventure*, "you are braver than you believe, stronger than you seem, and smarter than you think."

Here is a story, of unknown origin, that perfectly illustrates what persistence is all about:

There was a certain young man who went to meet a famous guru to ask the question, "which way is success?"

The wise old sage did not speak. Instead, he pointed to some place, far away in the distance. The man, delighted at the thought of quick success, took off in the appropriate direction. But, suddenly, there was a loud noise – a kind of "splat!" Eventually, the man staggered back, surprised and a bit bruised too. Assuming he must have misunderstood the instruction, he repeated his question. The guru again pointed silently in the same direction.

The man walked away once more and, after a little time, there was another loud "splat!" noise. When the man crawled back, he was stunned, hurt, and angry too.

"Hey" he shouted at the guru, "I asked you which way is success? I followed your directions and all I got was splatted! Will you quit all of this pointing malarkey and talk?"

Only then did the wise old man speak, and what he said was this: "Success *is* that way my friend, but it is a little further on than the splat!"

Translating your dream into a plan and then constantly taking actions, each and every day, that move you in the direction of your goal is what will get you there in the end. No matter how big you are aiming, you can succeed if you keep your destination in mind and then continually take actions that move you toward the goal.

When you meet an obstacle, as you inevitably will, persistence determines what you will do; whether you will give up or keep going. Persistence is what gets you back on your feet, dusted down and ready to go again.

Persistence is what gets you past SPLAT!

Flexibility

Flexibility: the quality of being adaptable

Flexibility: a measure of the ability to respond to changes in demand

1. Commitment
2. An Open Mind
3. Persistence
4. Flexibility
5. Faith
6. Thankfulness
7. Passion

It is a sound NLP (Neuro-Linguistic Programming) principle that to become successful, we need to notice what is working, and what is not, and be prepared to change our approach in order to get what we want - that is the essence of flexibility.

A wise person once said, "If you always do what you've always done, you'll always get what you've always got." That is a wonderfully true statement. In other words, if you continue doing exactly what you are now doing, then don't be surprised when you don't see any increase or change in your results.

It is the law of cause-and-effect in operation. The results you are now getting (effects) are the product of the causes (efforts) you have set in motion sometime in the past. To get greater benefits in the future, you need to change what you are doing in the present in order to produce them.

Whilst persistence is an important quality, persistence without flexibility can indeed be futile because, without some flexibility in your approach, you could end up trying to move an immovable object for the rest of your life. The willingness to constantly change what we are now doing and to also demonstrate persistence is what gets us around seemingly insurmountable obstacles.

So notice exactly what is working for you and notice what is not. Change your approach in some way - you will need to brainstorm various approaches - then continue to observe. But, by continually changing your approach and finding what works and what doesn't, you will literally become unstoppable.

As an example, consider the story of Kevin Keegan, the famous English footballer (soccer) and eventually, manager of the English national team. Kevin was told that he would never become a footballer because he was not talented enough, he was not strong enough and he was too small.

It would have been easy enough for him to just give up, after all, these people telling him he would never make it were all professionals. Surely they should have known what they were talking about. What did Kevin actually do? Well there was nothing he could do about his height, so he worked on what he could. He worked on his physique until he built a strong, powerful frame and he also worked on his basic ball skills.

After several trials, he was eventually signed as an apprentice for Scunthorpe United in 1967. He became a full professional twelve months later and, in 1971, moved to Liverpool F.C. where he played on the winning team in the F.A. Cup final (1974), the European Cup final (1977) and the UEFA Cup finals (1973 and 1976). He was also in the Liverpool team that won the Football League First Division title in two seasons (1972-3 and 1976-7).

Kevin eventually became the captain of England, winning 63 international caps between 1972 and 1982, and he became European Footballer of the Year in 1978 and 1979. He did it all by being flexible in his approach and persistent in the face of unfavourable odds.

Sometimes, I tell Kevin's story at my Workshop events and sometimes people will say something like this:

"What about all the people who tried and tried but still never made it?"

My answer is that Kevin would also have been another statistic along with the rest of them if he had not demonstrated these qualities. Kevin was a winner and you too can become a winner. To become a winner, you need to internalise the seven qualities we are discussing.

If you really want success, in whatever field of endeavour you are pursuing, you can have it - yes you can! But you need to be prepared to work for it - to do whatever it takes. Finding out and then doing *whatever it takes*, is the quality of flexibility.

Faith

Faith: acceptance of principles which are not necessarily demonstrable

Faith: strong belief in something without proof or evidence

1. Commitment
2. An Open Mind
3. Persistence
4. Flexibility
5. Faith
6. Thankfulness
7. Passion

There will be many people who will tell you that you will never, or simply cannot, achieve your dream. They are the 80% of people who once had a dream but have now settled for something less. They are the children who once stood in line at school, believing they would one day become pilots, doctors, actors, singers, ballerinas, novelists and so on.

But their experience of life gradually ground them down and their dreams were reluctantly put away. Those dreams still live somewhere, deep down within their hearts, but they no longer believe that they are achievable. A whole assortment of well-intentioned individuals inadvertently conspired to change their minds about what was realistic for them.

First, their parents worked on them, questioning their abilities, doubting their chances and telling them that they once had the same dreams. Their parents told them they needed to grow up, be more responsible and life would work out just great.

Then their teachers worked on them, saying that we all have such ambitions, but in the real world, you needed a trade, a job, a career - and that life had so very few of those exciting opportunities that you really wanted to know more about. They ingrained the attitude of the 'scarcity mentality' into their charges, rather than the 'abundance mentality'. They told these children that there just wasn't enough good stuff to go around.

Finally, their friends worked on them as they also settled for the jobs on offer. They questioned, what was so wrong with being a sales-person, a plumber, a secretary or a brick layer? The world needed these tradespeople (and so it does) and there was nothing wrong with making an honest living by providing these services.

That was how, gradually, their beliefs about the world were changed and they came to believe that it would not be possible to reach the heights they had once dreamed of, and so, they made their decision to settle for less; much less.

After all this negative conditioning, only a few of those pilots-in-the-making believed they could still learn to fly aircraft; only a few of those singers still believed they were destined to sing for their supper. Many people had their dream strangled out of them. And when you are once again ready to pursue what is in your heart, you need to be aware that you are still not immune to this kind of negativity. There will still be many people ready to tell you why what you are now doing, or about to do, is hopeless!

The problems begin when you believe what you are being told because our ability to perform is often limited by what we believe. But with faith in our ability to deal with the obstacles in our path, we are capable of overcoming seemingly overwhelming odds. As an example of what can be accomplished when you have faith in your own ability, consider the inspiring story of Glenn Cunningham.

As young boy, Glenn became trapped inside the school building when fire broke out. As a consequence, he was very badly burned and it seemed that he would die from his injuries as did his brother, Floyd. He lost the flesh from his legs and all of the toes from his left foot. The doctors recommended amputating his legs but, as he was so distressed, his parents would not agree to it.

Glenn survived, though, unfortunately from his waist down, he was left completely paralysed. However, determined to walk again, one day, he deliberately toppled his wheelchair causing him to fall to the ground. He then hauled his body across the front lawn to the fence at the edge of the garden where he painstakingly dragged himself along, post by post, all the while, trying to move his uncooperative legs.

He repeated this exercise every day, in the belief that he would one day be able to walk again, and his resolute persistence ultimately paid-off as he developed the ability, first to stand upright and then, after some time, to walk without assistance. But the story does not end there because this young man continued to progress. After a while, he started to walk to school, and then he even began running; first, just to school and back, but in due course, he was able to join the track team.

As inconceivable as it might seem for someone so badly injured, he eventually became a top-class athlete and, at Madison Square Garden, in February 1934, that same young man who had been paralysed, following a tragic accident that he had barely survived, broke the world record for the one mile event.

It is truly amazing what you can do when you believe in your own ability. That's why you need faith - a deep down, dogged belief that, regardless of the evidence, you are going to make it! You are going to achieve what you have set out to accomplish. You are going to make a difference in this life.

Thankfulness

Thankfulness: a virtue and a dynamic - activates the *Law of Attraction*

Thankfulness: a positive emotion involving a feeling of indebtedness

1. Commitment
2. An Open Mind
3. Persistence
4. Flexibility
5. Faith
6. Thankfulness
7. Passion

Attitude affects so many things in life. Sales-people are told they must maintain a positive mental attitude because it ultimately affects their sales, sports-people are told to cultivate a winner's attitude because it affects their performance. The laws of success tell us to cultivate a *grateful* attitude but why should thankfulness affect our success?

It may be difficult, at first, to see exactly how thankfulness (or gratitude) can be such an important key to your success, but by seeking to maintain an 'attitude of gratitude' you are indeed tapping into the timeless laws of success.

Thankfulness is fundamentally related to positivity and negativity. It is so much easier to be positive about your life and the things that are going on in it right now when you are grateful. As A. W. Tozer once commented, 'a thankful heart cannot be cynical'.

The workplace is full of people who are cynical; ready to run the company down, run the boss down and run the industry down and, do you know something? They can, and do, actually produce the evidence that supports their beliefs. Such people are also employing the laws of success but, by talking about what they do *not* like, they are using the principles to attract what they don't want. Their reality simply reinforces their views about the company, the boss, the industry and whatever else has been the subject of their negativity.

On the other hand, having an *attitude of gratitude* impacts your countenance and your general outlook on life and people, generally, will prefer to work with happy, cheerful, grateful people rather than miserable, downcast, merchants of doom and gloom. As a consequence, truly grateful people, literally attract opportunities that others miss or even possibly repel.

To help acquire this positive attitude, consider the idea of keeping a Gratitude Journal. Would you, every day for a period of one month, be prepared to actually write down all the things for which you are grateful? You know: count your blessings, the way you were taught as a child. As an example, you can take a look at the first few days of my own journal in the *appendix*.

What do you think might be the result of engaging in such an exercise? Consider the results of a scientific study into the subject. Two psychologists, McCollough and Emmons, conducted a study on the subject of gratitude and thanksgiving. In the study, three different groups of people were required to keep daily journals.

The first group kept a simple diary of all the events that occurred during the day, the second group kept a record of only their unpleasant daily experiences. The final group made a daily list of everything for which they were grateful i.e. they kept a Gratitude Journal.

The results of this amazing study suggested that the exercise of daily gratitude resulted in higher levels of alertness, enthusiasm, determination, optimism and energy. So let it really sink-in ...

- A Grateful Heart Cannot be Cynical.

- Gratitude is Fundamental to Maintaining an Optimistic Outlook.

- The Exercise of Thankfulness activates the *Law of Attraction*.

Additionally, the *gratitude* group experienced less depression and stress, and they were much more likely to get involved in helping others. They also exercised more regularly and made more progress toward their personal goals. Isn't that amazing? Just by keeping a Gratitude Journal, the study suggests, they were able to positively impact their chances of achieving their goals!

Thankfulness is an *attitude* and an important key to success. It is an attitude we all need to learn to acquire and apply in living our lives. It is not only about remembering to say thank you when someone has helped you out (as your mum, no doubt, will have taught you) although 'as a little bird once told me' that is a very important lesson too. Actually, let me tell you about that.

There was an occasion when I was out walking with a friend when we heard the sound of a bird signalling an alarm. Although our attention was attracted to the bird that was sitting in a shrub within a nearby garden, neither of us at first gave it much thought.

As we continued for a few more steps, the little bird remained very agitated and continued to blast out the same alarm call. My friend asked what I thought might be the problem and I thought that perhaps there might have been a cat somewhere close. However, she decided to go over to the garden to investigate.

The garden had a little wall with a wrought iron fence on top and it was possible to see through the fence. There on the path, a magpie had pinned down a sparrow and was repeatedly hacking at the bird with its beak. My friend quickly clapped her hands a few times and both birds immediately flew away.

What happened next is what has stayed with me all these years. The sparrow then flew down and landed in a shop doorway, just to our right. He bobbed his head a couple of times and then he flew off. My friend immediately commented that it was very nice of him to come and say *thank you*. I really have no idea what goes on in the mind of a sparrow but that's exactly what it seemed like.

From time to time, if ever we walk that same way, one of us might ask, "do you remember that little sparrow?" We are still both amazed at what happened. Could the bird have actually been saying thank you? It may be more likely that he was just a bit disorientated after a severe pecking and had simply flown off in the wrong direction. His apparent bob of the head could have just been him coming to terms with the headache that the magpie had given him. But you try telling my friend that. As far as she is concerned, in its own way, that little bird said thank you.

We did not notice the other bird; the one that had raised the alarm and persisted even though, at first, there did not seem to be any help arriving. But he really had saved the life of this little fellow through his action. Even though he could not take on the magpie himself, he was still able to change the situation.

There are some great lessons in there for us. Firstly, in difficult situations, where you feel helpless, you should at least do whatever you can; who knows what might turn up as a consequence? Second, if you don't get what you need right away, don't give up. Thirdly, if someone helps you out, make sure you remember to say *thank you* – it can go a long way.

But remember too, that saying thank you should not be *exclusively* reserved for those situations in which you have been helped. Whether or not you decide to keep your own Gratitude Journal, start to notice what those around you are already doing – friends, loved-ones, colleagues - often without any thought of personal reward, and be grateful for them. If you can learn to make gratitude a part of the way you live your life, you will be simply amazed at how the attitude of the people around you will change too.

Passion

Passion: strong, enthusiastic devotion to a cause, ideal, or goal

Passion: your heart's one true desire or the deepest desire of your heart

1. Commitment
2. An Open Mind
3. Persistence
4. Flexibility
5. Faith
6. Thankfulness
7. Passion

It is impossible to think about passion without reference to the heart. Deep within your heart, there is a desire, the pursuit of which will bring you all the happiness, success and fulfilment you really want. To find your passion is to identify your own unique purpose in life; to live your passion is to achieve what I like to refer to as the *Deepest Desire of Your Heart*.

You can achieve whatever you want. You can be the person you were meant to be and you can really live the life of your dreams. Those are bold statements but they are true and more and more people are discovering this wonderful truth for themselves. But if this is indeed true, then why is it that so many people - we think the figure is around 80% - are pursuing jobs and careers they don't really care about?

For our parents and grandparents, growing up in a world with comparatively few opportunities, it is true to say that their lives were consumed with the whole business of 'making a living' - looking after what Abraham Maslow called their physiological and social needs. They worked hard and never really enjoyed the luxury of considering what might be termed the 'higher needs' of the human condition.

Many people in today's workplace are indeed seeking to reach higher and often people think they have reached their peak when they have started to meet their 'esteem' needs, that is, the basic human need for respect, recognition and responsibility. For many people, this means pursuing an interesting career rather than just getting a job.

However, for very many people, there is still an inner emptiness. Often, this emptiness is experienced more starkly when they have actually become successful in their chosen careers. They start to wonder exactly what life has been about. The trappings of success: promotion, automobile and house did not bring about the happiness they anticipated. This is a consequence, as Stephen Covey puts it, of climbing the ladder of success only to find when they reach the top that, all along, the ladder has been leaning against the wrong wall.

To really achieve success in life, you must be bold enough to go even higher; to consider what Maslow called *Self Actualisation*. This means becoming the person you were meant to be and living the life you were meant to live. To do this, you need to discover your true self and start living your life in that knowledge. Only by doing this, can you possibly hope to find the success you really desire.

Once upon a time, a poultry farmer placed an eagle's egg in amongst his chickens to see what would happen. One of the chickens sat on the egg and nurtured it until, one day, it hatched and an eaglet was born. It grew up with the other chickens in the farmyard, scratching about and pecking at the earth. One day, the young eagle caught sight of a magnificent bird confidently soaring high in the sky, and he turned to an old rooster.

"What kind of bird is that?" he asked.

The old bird said, "that is an eagle, the most powerful bird in the land."

"I wish I could soar like that," the eagle said.

"But you can't," replied the chicken. "He is an eagle and we are just chickens."

And so, the eagle went back to scratching the ground and he lived the rest of his life like a chicken, for that is what he *believed* he was.

My friend, you are an eagle! You were born to fly, you are destined to soar. You are called to achieve something important with your life. Don't waste your opportunity.

There is No Failure

"Failure should be our teacher, not our undertaker. Failure is delay, not defeat. It is a temporary detour, not a dead end. Failure is something we can avoid only by saying nothing, doing nothing, and being nothing." - Denis Waitley

If there is one certain truth concerning the possibility of failure, it is that you cannot fail if you never attempt anything. None of us like to fail and perhaps, more than anything else, it is the fear of failing that holds many people back from defining their dream and going for it. Let's face it, it is a lot easier to just go with the flow, turn up, get paid and settle for living a quiet, untroubled existence.

At some time, you might come to think that you will never be able to reach your most ambitious goals, and that perhaps you were silly to even think it might be a possibility in the first place. That sentiment is essentially self-doubt, and if you experience it, it is really a *healthy* indicator that you are thinking in the right way. If you are dreaming big dreams, you are certain to have doubts about your own ability to succeed. All successful people have experienced self-doubt at some time in their journey to success.

Filled with self-doubt, many people are prepared to give up. They justify their decision by reasoning that there is nothing wrong with living a quiet life. The sad thing is that, in making that decision, they also are sacrificing their one opportunity to make a real difference in this world. But, at least, they don't have to worry about the effort of trying and therefore, never have to face the prospect of failure. As the saying goes, 'show me a person who has never failed and I will show you someone who has never tried!'

So what happens if you try and then, you fail? It is a very good question and one that is worth thinking about before you commence your journey. It is often also said that you cannot fail if you never give up. This is the essence of *persistence*, of course, but as we discussed earlier, you need to develop the wisdom to ensure you don't get into a situation where you are so invested in some approach that you won't let it go, even when everything is telling you it is not working.

Always remember that staying *flexible* means being prepared to change your approach to produce the result you are after. In changing your route, you are not changing the goal. Failure can be an excellent teacher in this respect, provided you are prepared to learn the lessons and ensure you don't repeat the same mistakes. As the NLP (Neuro-Linguistic Programming) principle puts it, 'there is no failure, only feedback.'

If you always view failure as the empirical evidence that some particular *idea*, *method* or *way* is not right, then you will be able to continually make adjustments to your approach, until you find what does work. This is the mentality of really successful people and it is the right way to deal with failure. If you fail, always try to learn from the experience.

When you are heavily invested in the success of a particular project, perhaps having even staked everything you have on its success, and it turns sour, then you are into the kind of territory that very few people have ever trod. That's the kind of experience that shaped some of the greatest successes in history. It is by learning from the experience that so few people can ever gain, that loftier goals and better plans can be forged. Yes, you will have to get up off the floor and try again. You will lick your wounds, think deeply about the experience and regroup.

Here are some questions to ponder when you find yourself in that place:

What have I learned through this experience?

What is the root cause of this failure?

How could this have been prevented?

What did I overlook?

What contingency might have saved the situation?

Where is the silver lining?

What am I taking away from this situation that will be invaluable in the future?

When you fail, as difficult as it may be, you should really welcome it. Of course, that's not an easy thing to do, but that attitude does separate the winners from the losers. Failure shapes us in a way that no other experience really can. You only have to study the lives of the people you admire the most to discover how they often failed their way to success.

We all know that 'a winner never quits and a quitter never wins' – that, I believe was something that Napoleon Hill once said. But there is a lot more to it than that. This is about learning the lessons that only those people who have ever stood where you are, right at that very moment, will *ever* have the opportunity to learn.

You can really only ever appreciate the vital importance of some of your failures after you have finally succeeded. Looking back, you will be able to see that you would never have been able to overcome some situation had you not previously experienced failure. Remember that success will be all the sweeter when it comes. Stay committed, but also make sure you learn from every failure.

There is one particular learning experience that I will always remember. It took place when I was about eleven years old and it lasted a couple of weeks. It was a very painful experience too. It was learning how to ride my bike.

The bicycle had been a Christmas present from my Grandmother. We didn't have a car in those days and we went to see my grandparents that year during the holidays. They lived in Scunthorpe (UK) and we got there using a mixture of taxis and the train. You can imagine what it was like bringing the bike back with us using the same services. I can remember other people telling my Dad that 'they' might not allow the bike on the train and that he would not be able to fit it into a taxi.

But he never allowed minor detail like that to get in the way.

Of course, the bike had to go away until Christmas day, but then, as soon as I could get my hands on it, me and my Mum were out front, ready to give riding it a shot. She had a simple plan: I was to sit on the bike whilst she held onto the back of the saddle. She was going to hold on to keep me steady while I pedalled. What she didn't tell me was that she was going to let go when we were up to a little speed. In her mind, I would not know the difference; I would be happily pedalling away and riding the bicycle and she would have successfully passed on this important skill.

So, it was probably about three or four seconds later that I crashed into the neighbour's fence, falling from my bike and badly grazing my knee. Ouch! I can still feel that fall now. "Right," she announced, completely unperturbed by the circumstances, "get back on." Well, I thought she had to be joking, but she wasn't. I think it took a bit of encouraging before I was prepared to give it another go, but I can remember her telling me that everyone falls off the first time and now it was going to be all okay.

It wasn't! I still have the school photograph, taken a couple of days later showing me with the two black eyes. It was one of the most painful moments of my young life. I remember that the neighbour came out and picked me up. He carried me back home and my Mum cleaned me up. There was this stuff they used to put on cuts back in those days - iodine - ouch, again! And I can still feel the sting of that stuff too.

In those days, when you bought something for a child, especially clothing as I recall, you always bought the item that was a few sizes too big and then the child wore the garment until it was a few sizes too small. Children grow so quickly and that was the way you could ensure you got your money's worth. My Gran naturally bought into this philosophy, so the bike was too big for me. My Dad put blocks on the pedals so that I could reach them, but as I recall, I could just about get my tip toes on the ground if I got off the saddle and straddled the crossbar. That meant that there really was no reliable way I could stop.

It was a couple of weeks later that my Mum thought I was ready for lesson number two. This time, she briefed me about what to do. She explained how to stay on and, as a result, I felt a lot more confident. But it was all to no avail as time and again, I fell off the thing.

But I remember the turning point. It was when I decided to practice using *her* bike. It was much bigger than mine, of course, but because it was a ladies bicycle, it had no crossbar and that meant that I could get my feet on the floor quickly, when I needed to. That made all the difference. Soon I was able to ride her bike without falling off and, once my brain had made the right connections, I was able to get back on my own bike and ride it, despite the aforementioned difficulties.

Sometimes life is just like that. We want to learn something, but we just have to, metaphorically, fall off.

We get hurt, we doubt ourselves and our courage takes a knock. When we are ready, we get back into the hot seat ready to give it another go and we fall off again. We begin to wonder just how many times we will have to pick ourselves up and try again before we start to get things right.

As I remember the late, great Jim Rohn saying on one occasion, succeeding is the same process that a baby goes though when they are learning to walk. They don't try a few times and then give up, they try and try and try (and try) *until* they can walk. In fact, anyone who has ever watched a baby learning this skill will know that they too, first learn how to fall (fail) safely ... and then they try and try until they succeed. What is going on inside their brain, with each apparent failure, is called *plasticity* – their infant brain is shaped and moulded through the experience. Subtle adjustments are being made with each apparent failure and that is how the necessary learning takes place.

The same applied when I learned to ride my bike. Using my Mom's bike meant that I could effectively fall (fail) without getting too badly hurt. So think about this, in relation to whatever you are trying to achieve because, when we fail, we naturally don't feel too good about ourselves; failure is often painful and we can easily get discouraged. But perhaps, before you can master that difficult task or skill, failure might not only be inevitable, it might actually be necessary.

Perhaps the best example of the use of failure as a feedback mechanism can be found in the story of

Thomas Edison who, as you know, invented the first practical electric lamp. The principle of generating light using electricity had been demonstrated by the Englishman, Sir Humphry Davy, in 1860. After that, the idea of producing a commercially practical electric light was worked on by the Englishman, Sir Joseph Wilson Swan, and Americans, Charles Francis Brush and Lewis H. Latimer. However, it was Thomas Edison, in 1879, who eventually managed to produce the first commercially viable electric lamp.

But, in the process, the amount of apparent failure that Edison had to endure before he finally found success was absolutely astonishing. He conducted thousands of unsuccessful experiments at his laboratory in Menlo Park, New Jersey, before he found exactly the right filament.

> "After we had conducted thousands of experiments on a certain project without solving the problem, one of my associates, after we had conducted the crowning experiment and it had proved a failure, expressed discouragement and disgust over our having failed to find out anything. I cheerily assured him that we had learned something. For we had learned for a certainty that the thing couldn't be done that way, and that we would have to try some other way."
>
> *Interview with Thomas Edison, published in the January 1921 issue of American Magazine.*

It is understandable and quite natural to become downhearted, discouraged and even, as Edison's associate had been, disgusted, following failure. On occasions, you might even feel like giving up. But you have to accept that your journey to success is inevitably going to pass through this territory at some stage and it is what you do, when you are in that place, that determines whether or not you will finally succeed.

The Journey to Success

Some people seem to be born with an innate sense of what they want to achieve in life, or they become aware of it when they are young. In many ways, they are very fortunate because with their destiny in mind, they have effectively already taken the first step towards success i.e. finding their own vocation or calling – their life-purpose. So they can go straight to the next step which, of course, is planning the route.

It seems that many successful people had this inner knowledge early on in life. As an example, consider the story of Ian Callum which was the subject of a short BBC film. From the age of just three years old, he says, he knew he wanted to design things, and as he got a little older, he realised it was cars that he wanted to design. At fourteen years old, he wrote a letter to the head of design at Jaguar Cars. He got a reply that provided advice on how to become a designer. It recommended subjects he would need to study and qualifications he should obtain. So he allowed that advice to become his blueprint for success, and eventually, he actually managed to become the head of design at Jaguar Cars.

Ian's is an amazing story that shows how really successful people often have that sense of vocation very early in life, and it is by no means an isolated example of the phenomenon. As a child, I remember watching the 1963 F.A. Cup Final between Manchester United and Leicester City, which United won by three goals to one. During the game, the commentator, Kenneth Wolstenholme, mentioned something that had been written on the Manchester United winger, David Herd's school report by his Headmaster.

"David will never earn a living playing football."

Not only did David Herd prove his Headmaster to be completely wrong, he actually scored two of the three goals that won the cup for United that day.

Here's another example.

As with many successful bands, it began with two kids playing guitar together as often as they possibly could. On one occasion, just before they were about to sit their final exams, the two youngsters were found playing guitar at school, when they were supposed to have been studying.

The teacher angrily admonished them, "if you two don't start getting your act together, you are going to be in *dire straits*!" It turned out that they thought that would be a good name for their new band – you might have heard of them.

For people who never had that degree of clarity or perhaps, simply had no idea what they wanted to do with their lives at the beginning of their journey, the route to success is usually more circuitous. But such people can still manage to find success once they have identified their life-purpose.

Here are a few examples of people who took a little time to discover their true passion:

Leonard Cohen struggled as a folk performer until he made the decision to start performing his own songs. After releasing his first album *The Songs of Leonard Cohen*, when he was 30, his career took off.

Andrea Bocelli graduated from law school at the age of 30 and took a job as an attorney. After a year, he gave it up to pursue his love of singing. Three years later, he found outstanding success.

Vera Wang was a professional figure skater who competed twice at the US National Championships. She changed direction and went on to work at Vogue. Within a year, at the age of 23, she became the youngest ever senior fashion editor at the magazine.

There are many other people who 'found their voice' much later in life. But having that vision - that clarity of purpose - is the real starting point. If you don't have absolute clarity about what you want to achieve, it does not mean that you won't ever develop it. However, if you want to be successful, your first priority should be to identify your own life-purpose.

Once you understand who you are and why you are here, you can move on to the next part of the journey which involves planning your mission and setting the goals that will take you there. These goals are not just plucked out of the air; they are specific steps that will take you to where you want to be.

As your journey to success progresses, you will need to internalise the seven keys we have discussed. To *internalise* means to make these principles a part of yourself and you do that by practice.

It is only after you have identified your life-purpose, that you can possibly *commit* yourself to achieving it. But that step alone will make such a big difference to your life. After that you can apply the qualities of *persistence*, *flexibility* and *passion* to the creation and execution of your plan, whilst developing a winning attitude that embraces *receptiveness* (open-mindedness), *faith* and *thankfulness* (gratitude).

One of the most interesting insights into success and what it means can come about by actually meeting some highly successful people. Successful people, we discover, are more like ourselves than we might have at first imagined. They had an ambitious dream, they were filled with self-doubt and they suffered failure. But they applied the seven principles we have been discussing to develop their fundamental character and become winners.

There is nothing more certain than the truth that you will achieve *your* dream if you first allow yourself to dream it and then, apply the principles that are outlined in this little book.

Spiritual Principles

Perhaps it is worth mentioning that numerals hold special significance within many religious and cultural traditions. The number seven was considered to be a divine number from the earliest times, way back in the religious traditions of ancient Egypt, but is also significant within all major world religions today.

In the Christian tradition, the number seven represents perfection or completeness. So it seems fitting that we have exactly that number of principles in our list. The following references, which are some of my favourites, are provided as examples but are by no means the only places these seven success principles can be found in The Bible.

Commitment

> Commit your way to the LORD and trust in Him, and He will act. – Psalm 37:5

An Open Mind (Receptiveness)

> Ask, and it will be given to you; seek, and you will find; knock, and it will be opened to you. - Matthew 7:7

Persistence

> I have fought the good fight, I have finished the race, I have kept the faith. - 2 Timothy 4:7

Flexibility

> I prefer a flexible heart to an inflexible ritual - *The Message*, Matt 12:6

Faith

> If you have faith, the size of a mustard seed, you can say to this mountain, 'Move from here to there,' and it will move. Nothing will be impossible for you. – Matthew 17:20

Thankfulness (Gratitude)

> Rejoice always, pray continually, give thanks in all circumstances - 1 Thessalonians 5:16-18

Passion

> He will grant your heart's desire and fulfil all your plans. – Psalm 20:4

Of course, the principles we have been discussing need not be connected or concerned with spiritual development at all. However, if there's one thing that characterises the genre today, it is the recognition that forming some kind of connection with a higher plane of existence is, in some way, fundamentally connected with the process of personal development.

Some writers, including myself, prefer to use the term 'God' in describing this personal connection, but many others prefer alternative labels, such as 'the universe' or 'the collective mind' or 'creative consciousness'. Personally, I have no difficulty with any of these terms since I simply see each of them as attributes of God. Furthermore, when we take on the task of becoming the person we need to be, in order to reach our most important goals, I believe that we are essentially engaging in God's business for our lives.

In Christian tradition, the process of personal growth describes adding characteristics such as *virtue, knowledge, temperance, patience, godliness, brotherly kindness* and *love* to our character (2 Peter). Other religious traditions teach similar concepts to those addressed in personal development literature. For example, consider the four 'factors of fulfilment' from Buddhism: *wealth, worldly satisfaction, spirituality* and *enlightenment*. In my workshops, I am sometimes informed by delegates that the concepts are also wholly represented within Islam.

The late Stephen Covey said that the seven habits outlined in his book were to be found in every major world religion. Exactly the same is true of the seven success principles we have been studying. Religious teaching from many traditions, if divided on lesser issues, seems to be completely unified on many of the greater issues relating to the human condition concerning what will bring us happiness and how we should relate to our fellow humans, which is (just in case you missed it) with love.

God is much bigger than religion and he is in the business of personal transformation. In other words, your own personal growth and the process of becoming the person you need to be, in order to reach your goals, is a spiritual process that is fundamentally connected with finding and achieving your life-purpose. And that, I personally believe, is God-given.

Universal Principles

Successful people throughout history have discovered and applied the *seven keys* to create astonishing levels of success in their lives. The following quotations, which are some of my favourites, affirm the importance of these universal success principles.

Commitment

"Commitment unlocks the doors of imagination, allows vision, and gives us the right stuff to turn our dream into reality." - James Womack

An Open Mind (Receptiveness)

"Do the thing and you will be given the power." - Ralph Waldo Emerson

Persistence

"Let me tell you the secret that has led to my goal. My strength lies solely in my tenacity." – Louis Pasteur

Flexibility

"Stay committed to your decisions, but stay flexible in your approach." –Tony Robbins

Faith

"Faith is taking the first step even when you don't see the whole staircase." - Martin Luther King, Jr.

Thankfulness (Gratitude)

> "When I started counting my blessings, my whole life turned around." - Willie Nelson

Passion

> "There is no passion to be found playing small - in settling for a life that is less than the one you are capable of living." - Nelson Mandela

It is difficult to say when the first self-help, or personal development, book was written. There are a number of ancient books which might be considered as candidates including, for example, the book of *Proverbs* from The Bible. Certainly, by the time of the great Greek philosophers, many of the principles we would now recognize as basic self-help tenets, including the importance of goal-setting, had been proposed; indeed some by Aristotle himself.

In America, self-help material has been in existence since the time of the *Declaration of Independence*. It is perhaps not surprising when you look at some of the principles enshrined in that document.

> We hold these truths to be self-evident, that all men are created equal, that they are endowed by their Creator with certain unalienable Rights, that among these are Life, Liberty and the pursuit of Happiness.
>
> *The Declaration of Independence of the Thirteen Colonies. In CONGRESS, July 4, 1776*

Those ideas contrast markedly with the dominant attitude in Europe, at that time, which is best summed up in the theory of the *Divine Right of Kings*. This theory extends well backwards into time and has probably been around as long as monarchy itself.

> Jacques-Benigne Bossuet (1627-1704) reinforced medieval notions of kingship in his theory of the Divine Right of Kings, a theory which argued that certain kings ruled because they were chosen by God to do so and that these kings were accountable to no person, except God.
>
> *The European Enlightenment Glossary*

Basically, in Europe up to the time of its revolutions, we thought that it was not the place of ordinary men and women to entertain ideas such as self-advancement. However, today we live in much more enlightened times in which many people are bold enough to believe that we can actually create our own reality and that our quality of life is largely a matter of choice. Irrespective of where we were born, and regardless of the circumstances, successful people throughout history have adopted these seven principles to change their lives for the better.

Accepting personal responsibility for your own life is, in my view, a hallmark of the adult character. It is an acceptance of the fact that life is *not* fair, and a subsequent taking-on of the responsibility for where your own life will take you. It is completely accepting that we didn't all get the same start in life and that the odds may be stacked in favour of some people who don't realise just how privileged they are, but that the remainder of the script for *your* life has not yet been written.

The Rest of Your Life

"The people who are crazy enough to think they can change the world are the ones who do." – Steve Jobs

There is a synergy between the principles listed above that causes them to produce an effect that is so much greater than the sum of the individual parts. This may not be entirely apparent at first, but if you diligently work at applying these methods, your life will certainly change for the better – that is the minimum you can expect. But the heights to which you might climb as you begin to impact the world around you, might truly astonish you.

You can make a difference, right where you are and in whatever line of business you choose to operate if you hold on to your vision and keep chipping away. It all begins with your own personal belief about what is possible. As Steve Jobs so insightfully said, you have to first *believe* you can change things.

One of the most difficult things for many people to take on board is that, very often, it is quite ordinary people who manage to achieve the most extraordinary things. Perhaps even more incredibly, as Alan Turing said, in the movie *The Imitation Game*, "sometimes it is the people no one can imagine anything of, who do the things no one can imagine."

Here are some examples:

Thomas Edison had very little formal education. He suffered hearing difficulties and was taught, at home, by his mother. But he went on to become America's greatest inventor.

Albert Einstein was the son of an engineer. He worked as a clerk in a patent office before developing the *theory of relativity*, which is regarded as one of the pillars of modern physics.

Michael Faraday was born to a very poor family and actually educated himself. He found work as a bookbinder, but went on to discover the principles of electromagnetism.

Mohandas (Mahatma) Gandhi was born into a Hindu *merchant caste* (class) family. He went on to lead India to independence and inspired civil rights movements across the world.

Louis Pasteur was the son of a poor tanner. He became a biologist and eventually discovered the principles of vaccination, microbial fermentation and pasteurization.

You might think that these people were in some kind of different league to yourself, but that is only because of what they managed to achieve. In all other respects, they were ordinary people from quite unremarkable backgrounds. So let it sink in: ordinary people, just like you and me, can and do achieve extraordinary things.

You are a truly unique person: you can tell this simply by taking a moment or two to look at your thumb print. Do that now – go on, humour me – take a look at your thumb print and know this: you are the *only* person who has ever lived, to have that thumb print! Isn't that truly amazing? In fact, it is even more amazing than that because, as it turns out, you are the only person who will *ever* have that thumb print.

So you already know, in your heart that you are unique. You are not only unique, you are talented too, even if you don't think you are. You have at least one talent that makes you better than anyone else at some specific thing. Sure, I know this may be difficult to accept, at least, at first, and especially if you have not yet discovered your talent.

But it is true: you *do* have some unique gift or a unique expression of a specific gift - something that enables you to make an important contribution. Don't pay any attention to those who tell you otherwise. The following story illustrates why you need to be very careful about what unqualified people say.

One day, a bunch of frogs decided to have a race to see if anyone could get to the top of a tall tree. As the race started, some of the other frogs in the crowd began to comment,

"Oh, they'll never make it."

"That tree is just too tall for a frog to climb."

"They don't have a chance."

Many of the frogs fell back to the ground, but a small group continued the race. The crowd still did not believe they would be able to make it and you could hear them saying,

"They are all going to get hurt."

"They are all way too high."

"This really is far too dangerous."

And, sure enough, the remaining frogs all fell from the tree – all but one, that is. He made it all the way to the very top and, when they asked that outstandingly successful frog how he managed to achieve the seemingly impossible feat and actually climb that tall tree, he answered ...

"Pardon?"

It turned out ... that the winner was stone deaf which, in this situation, turned out to be a very good thing.

Very often, other people will have opinions about what you are attempting to do and very often, they will turn out to be negative opinions, especially if you are trying to accomplish anything challenging. Perhaps, one of life's greatest lessons is to learn to not take heed of other people's negativity. Everyone will have an opinion whether or not they are qualified to give it. If you want an opinion on something, find an expert in that field. Don't listen to the myriad opinions of the unqualified majority. Instead, be like that super-frog and just keep going.

Remember that you are here only once and this is your life - right now. Do not make the mistake of believing that life holds no purpose for you. You are called to achieve something significant with your life. So start by identifying your true *life-purpose* and then find the courage to begin living the life you were born to live. This is the unfailing path that will bring outstanding success to you. And, no matter what anyone else thinks, you *can* do it!

Changing the World

One time when my daughter was very young, perhaps about five years old, we went on holiday to Portugal. We spent many happy hours there on the beach; her catching small fish and crabs in her plastic bucket and me just taking it easy, playing with her, doing a bit of swimming and reading a few books. One day, she found a starfish that had been baked hard in the sun. We looked at it together, marvelling at how wonderful these creatures are, and then I finally tossed it aside on the beach and got back to reading my book.

However, she retrieved the starfish, filled her Frisbee with sea water and put the little fellow in there. After about an hour or so, she brought the Frisbee over to announce that the starfish was alive. Of course, I had previously seen it as stiff as a board and so, at first, I thought this was her childhood imagination at work. But she pointed out that the fish was laying toward the edge of the Frisbee, in the shadow. She then turned the Frisbee to expose the fish to the sunlight and, very slowly, the starfish made its way back to the shadow on the other side. I could hardly believe it, but he was indeed alive.

With the delightful exuberance of a five year old, she then asked if she could keep him as a pet; she have already given him a name, *Charlie*. After I had explained why she couldn't, I told her that we would need to throw him back into the sea to give him a chance to live a long and happy life with all of the other fishes. She then asked me if she could keep him, for just for one night, in the hotel. Well, I thought she had earned the right, so I agreed to her request. She brought some fresh sea water in her bucket, we took him back to the hotel and she looked after him that evening, as best as she could, with such limited resources.

The next day, we took Charlie down to the harbour where the water was deepest and I threw him as far as I could out to sea. We both felt really pleased that she had saved him and given him a second chance. She has now grown up, has a daughter of her own, and has probably forgotten all about the incident. But one day, when an angel shows her what life would have been like if she had not been born (like in the movie *It's a Wonderful Life*) I feel sure that in some way, the spirit of that little starfish will be there to thank her.

Sometimes, we may feel that there is just so much wrong with the world that we cannot possibly make a positive difference. But, as my daughter taught me that day, the world can be changed by ordinary people just like you and me. Doing whatever we can, we metaphorically become starfish throwers, changing the world one day at a time, one idea at a time, one act at a time. As Mother Theresa once so beautifully put it, "if you can't feed a hundred people, then feed just one."

Our mission (at White Dove Books) is to change the world, one book at a time, by helping people to develop their own unique talents, abilities and passion in order that they may lead more joyful, meaningful and fulfilled lives. Just imagine what would happen if millions of people were to decide to start living the lives they were born to live - just think of the amazing transformation that would result. The most astonishing power, operating for good, would be unleashed within the world if a substantial number of individuals committed themselves to achieving their unique calling. My hope is that *you* will be one of those people.

If you would like to help us to achieve *our* ambitious goal, all that is necessary is for you to recommend this book to someone who you think would benefit. That really is all that is necessary because the message will naturally multiply if you will help and, eventually, it will touch the hearts and minds of those people who need to hear its message. So, if you have enjoyed reading and would like to help, please pass the message on. Isn't it exciting to be a part of something that can change the world?

In closing, I would like to thank you for reading. My hope is that you have become convinced that life holds a specific purpose for you. The most important thing you can do is to find your true purpose, develop your vision and go for it, and whatever it is that *you* are here to achieve, may your own personal journey to success be filled with joy and happiness.

More by Will Edwards

Born and raised in Liverpool, Will attended the 'tough old school' he wrote about in his first novel *Fergus and Me*. Completing the formal part of his education, he graduated from the University of Birmingham, and travelled the world with the British company Apricot International where he was Technical Manager.

Now enjoying the privilege of being able to write full time, he is committed to producing books that inspire and challenge people to live more rewarding and fulfilling lives. If you enjoyed this book, you are sure to like his other books too; you can get them here:

<u>www.whitedovebooks.com</u>

These days, he lives in a converted old barn nestled into the beautiful Exe Valley in the English county of Devon where he does most of his thinking, walking and writing. In his spare time, he likes to write songs and he can often be seen singing and playing guitar or piano at local musical events.

Appendix A: Gratitude Journal

7 Days of Gratitude – My Gratitude Journal

Do you remember what you were taught at Sunday School; that when you begin to count your blessings, you will be surprised at just how many there are? Here is the little chorus I remember that we used to sing as children:

Count your blessings, name them one by one,
Count your blessings, see what God has done.
Count your many blessings, name them one by one,
And it will surprise you what the Lord has done.

– Johnson Oatman, Jr

The power of gratitude is unleashed into our lives in ways that may not be immediately apparent. I have become convinced that learning to develop an *attitude-of-gratitude* is fundamentally connected with achieving success. Perhaps this is something that you might consider doing too. Once you start the list, it will probably surprise you that there are just so many things that need to go on there.

Day 1 of My Gratitude Journal

Recognising that there are just so many things to list and understanding that I will not be able to list everything right now, here is the start of my list of things for which I am grateful:

When I look at this beautiful planet upon which we live, I feel I want to start by saying that I am grateful for life itself. I am grateful for having lived and enjoyed all the wonderful pleasures that life has to offer, discovering the joy of learning and the finding the opportunity to create something that will outlive me.

Secondly, I am grateful for my lovely wife, Amy. I am grateful for everything she has done for me in our life together including believing in me, supporting my efforts and providing me with my most trusted and valued source of help and good counsel.

I am grateful for all my close relationships. To my parents, both of whom have now passed on, I am grateful for everything they did for me. They always had my best interests at heart and always acted in the best possible way. I am grateful to my sister who is one of the kindest, most unselfish and good-hearted people I have ever known. And I am grateful to my kids, both of whom have turned out to be kind, caring and genuine people that I am proud to call my children. I am grateful for all my good friends with whom I have 'chewed the cud' and shared so much of life and its pleasures.

For the important lessons I have learned, I am grateful to everyone that I found *difficult* during my entire working career. Since God knows that I still have not learned, well enough, the practice of patience, the art of empathy and the ability to respect opinions, I expect that he will be lining up a few more such people for me to learn from in the future. I want to change my attitude toward anyone that I find difficult, and be grateful for each new relationship, treating them as wonderful opportunities for personal growth.

I am grateful for the privilege of having known some very special people including Cornel Munn who is a truly exceptional person. Born without arms and with just one leg, this person has achieved so much with his life that I don't have space to begin to list his achievements here. But I am grateful for receiving such an object lesson in what can be achieved through determination, persistence and effort. Another exceptional person I met is Jennifer Cox, who is involved in helping to support an orphanage in Honduras. I am grateful for the opportunity to have helped, in some small way, and learned in the process that what really makes me happy is helping others.

I am grateful to have finally found my life purpose and to have a vision and mission that gives my life meaning and focus. It is a real joy and a privilege to be actually doing what I envisioned all those years ago when I imagined myself as a writer, simply engaging in my writing as my own contribution to life. I am grateful for the enduring good health I have enjoyed and the ability to think and problem-solve that is vitally important for me to achieve my mission and important goals.

Writing is, necessarily, a solitary business and I actually love that solitude, but it is also very nice to connect with readers, so I want to say that I am grateful to you, dear reader. I am grateful for the people who find my books and enjoy reading what I write. I am grateful for the many positive comments and emails I receive about what I am doing.

So that's the start of my gratitude list. As the Johnson Oatman chorus said, there are so many things that we can be grateful for, when we stop to think about them, and I feel that the process of simply listing these things has been very beneficial to me.

Day 2 of My Gratitude Journal

I Am Grateful for:

My dog, who is always so pleased to see me, and who reminds me that I am also supposed to treat every person I meet as if they are the most important person in the world.

My critics, who remind me that I am far from perfect and help me to understand why my work on improving myself will never actually finish.

Music that inspires me and uplifts my spirit, helping me to understand why I know that there is more to life than we can appreciate in this iteration of our experience.

Laughter, the medicine that infects me and convulses my body, healing me and causing me to remember what it was like to be a child.

Language that gives expression to the beauty of the human spirit and provides the mechanism to directly connect with another person's heart.

Great art that challenges me to see things from an alternative perspective and helps me to understand that there really is no correct view of anything.

The stars that reveal the true magnitude and splendour of the creation within which we live and remind me just how tiny and insignificant we are in the grand order of things.

The flowers in my garden that perennially brighten up my life, elicit powerful associations by their evocative scents and remind me that life is a continuous cycle.

Local squirrels that move in the most wonderful undulating sine waves, fend for themselves and teach me that we live in a truly abundant world.

Butterflies that migrate half way around the world, helping us to understand the astonishing power in grace and gentleness, and showing how life really can follow death.

Honey bees that live in perfect communities and demonstrate the essence of what can be achieved through the agency of a well organised society.

Day 3 of My Gratitude Journal

Today, my mind is very much on outdoor matters. Well, here goes.

I am grateful for:

Sunshine that holds the power to transform the mundane into the pleasant and the beautiful into the magnificent.

The sea that ebbs and flows with the cycles of the Moon, dancing or crashing its waves against the shore with the interplay of the seasons, reminding us of the continuous and unchanging nature of the rhythms of life.

The gentle breeze of a summer evening that calms, cools and invigorates, leaving the mind renewed, refreshed and ready for fresh thinking.

The sheer joy of walking through the most beautiful landscape, drinking in the scenery, having absolutely nothing better to do with my time and nowhere else I am required to be.

Wild flowers, those great opportunists that plant themselves in the most unlikely places, brightening the countryside and demonstrating the true abundance that is to be found everywhere in nature.

Birds, of every kind, that soar and swoop above, demonstrating complete mastery of their environment and reminding me of what it means to be truly free.

Trees, so beautifully adapted and shaped to their environment that they steadily become giants that stand majestically, quietly outliving generation after generation.

Wild animals that peek and sneak about the rugged countryside, their fleeting presence punctuating the undergrowth with dots of curious interest.

Day 4 of My Gratitude Journal

Today, as I sit here in my study, writing, my mind is focused on my immediate surroundings.

I am thankful for:

My beautiful home in the Exe Valley located in the most stunning verdant countryside of Devon, a seemingly forgotten corner of England, with its rolling hills and little villages that delight me at every turn. And the temperate, wet climate that makes this country such a beautiful place to live.

Living right now, in *this* time and not in any other. I cannot know the future, but I do know a little about the past and I genuinely believe that I was born for 'such as time as this' that gives me the best opportunity to be the person I was predestined to become.

The opportunity to do what I love. In order for me to be sitting here in the comfort of my study, writing books and independently publishing them through my own imprint (White Dove Books), the internet had to be invented, Amazon, Google, Apple, Barnes and Noble, Kobo and many other online businesses all needed to develop their offerings to create that wonderful possibility and it is really an amazing thing that such an opportunity actually exists today.

The working farm on which my barn is situated and the horses, sheep, cows and many other farm animals that continually graze the hills surrounding the valley within which I live, keeping the fields as neat and tidy as a freshly mowed lawn. And the farmers who, in addition to caring for their livestock, seed, feed and weed, cut and trim, tend and mend.

The many wild animals that are rarely seen (deer, foxes, hares, badgers, moles, mice, voles, stoats, weasels, shrews) but remain an important part of the local ecosystem. And those other wild animals that are much more visible, having managed to successfully integrate their lives with the activities of humans (bats, hedgehogs, squirrels) including the colony of playful rabbits that have invaded my garden to chew on the Hebes and eat my lawn.

My cheerful and friendly neighbours, who are always there to help whenever the need should arise, and the good folk of Devon wherever 'they are to' (a peculiarly West Country turn of phrase) who love this delightfully unspoiled place as much as I do.

Day 5 of My Gratitude Journal

Today, I want to list some of the important things that I may tend to simply take for granted.

I am grateful for:

The freedom to think, say and do, almost anything I choose, as long as I am not being inconsiderate or disrespectful to others. Many countries respect human liberty and dignity, but there are some governments that do not align their systems and practices with these basic human rights.

The basic necessities of life such as food on the table, a roof over our heads and, as Jack Dawson said in *Titanic*, 'air in my lungs'. When it comes down to it, we humans don't really need many things, but we do need those things. There are also many other things to which I never give a second thought, but are important for life in a developed society including the basic utilities: fresh water, fuel, power and so on, all available at the touch of a button or flick of a switch.

Strangers that show kindness and consideration toward other people, whether it is holding the door open for someone, buying a cup of coffee for a homeless person, helping a young mother with a pushchair to navigate the stairs or whatever else they do voluntarily and cheerfully, setting an example for us all.

Everyone who has ever influenced and/or inspired me personally, including my parents, my old English master (Mr Argent) and early mentor and friend, Allan Sherborne. I was also inspired by some of the great teachers such as Jim Rohn, Zig Ziglar and Stephen Covey (sadly, all now deceased) and some wonderful human beings such as Nelson Mandela, Tony Benn and Bobby Charlton who will *always* be a hero of mine.

Day 6 of My Gratitude Journal

Today, I am going to list everything I can think of, that I especially love, as they say, in no particular order.

I am grateful for:

Freshly-baked rye bread.

Fresh eggs from the farm.

English strawberries.

Peanut butter.

Football (the beautiful game).

All kinds of music.

All kinds of art.

Peace and quiet.

Beauty in all its forms.

Day 7 of My Gratitude Journal

Today, it seems appropriate to list of all the gifts (strengths) that God has bestowed upon me and for which I am especially grateful.

I am grateful for:

My ability to appreciate art.

My ability to play piano.

My ability to write songs.

My ability to write books.

My ability to think for myself.

My ability to solve problems.

My ability to teach.

My ability to adapt to circumstances.

My ability to feel the pain of others.

Well, that's about it for now, though I know that there is a lot more to come. I wonder if you will be encouraged to start your own gratitude journal. Perhaps you could give it a try and let me know how it made you feel. Remember that, as some wise person once said, "a grateful heart cannot be a hateful heart."

Appendix B: Success Quotes

As you might imagine, successful people are usually more than happy to give credit to the principles that brought them outstanding success. The following success quotations are some of my favourites:

"However difficult life may seem, there is always something you can do and succeed at." - Stephen Hawking

"Success is no accident. It is hard work, perseverance, learning, studying, sacrifice and most of all, love of what you are doing or learning to do" - Edson Arantes do Nascimento (Pele)

"Desire is the key to motivation, but its determination and commitment to an unrelenting pursuit of your goal - a commitment to excellence - that will enable you to attain the success you seek." - Mario Andretti

"Success does not consist in never making mistakes but in never making the same one a second time." - George Bernard Shaw

"Four things for success: work and pray, think and believe." - Norman Vincent Peale

"If one advances confidently in the direction of his dreams, and endeavours to live the life which he has imagined, he will meet with a success unexpected in common hours." - Henry David Thoreau

"You don't have to be a genius or a visionary or even a college graduate to be successful. You just need a framework and a dream." - Michael Dell

"I do not think that there is any other quality so essential to success of any kind as the quality of perseverance. It overcomes almost everything." - John D. Rockefeller

"I attribute my success to this: I never gave or took any excuse." - Florence Nightingale

"Treat failure as a lesson on how not to approach achieving a goal, and then use that learning to improve your chances of success when you try again. Failure is only the end if you decide to stop." - Richard Branson

"Many of life's failures are people who did not realize how close they were to success when they gave up." - Thomas A. Edison

"The size of your success is measured by the strength of your desire; the size of your dream; and how you handle disappointment along the way." - Robert Kiyosaki

The Back Story

The idea for *The 7 Keys to Success* arose when a working associate sent me a short, inspirational video that listed the seven success principles we have been discussing. That particular video is no longer available. But at the time, I enjoyed it very much and as a consequence, felt inspired to begin writing this book, filling it with anecdotes and personal stories to illustrate the seven important principles.

It was the early days of the web, before the Kindle and various other tablets and electronic readers had arrived on the scene. There were comparatively few opportunities for digital distribution back then. So I decided to publish the book and distribute it via my own website. Early versions are still floating around the web, but the most recent revision is now available from leading online bookstores including Amazon, Apple, Barnes & Noble, Google Play and Kobo.

It wasn't very long after its initial publication that people began writing to say the book had helped them to find courage, make necessary changes to their lives or perhaps, even begin their lifework. Then, as now, it is always a huge thrill to hear from people who have read the book, and with whom the message resonates. If you have enjoyed reading, it would be wonderful if you would leave a short review at the bookstore where you obtained your copy.

The text of *The 7 Keys to Success* has evolved somewhat, over the years, and is sure to continue to develop in the future. Something I would love to include in a future revision is the success stories of readers who have applied the principles.

If you would like to submit your story for possible inclusion in a future edition of this book, please send it to me (whitedovebooks@gmail.com). Your story should be about 500 words, which is about two pages in length and it should be something that will help, uplift or inspire other people. If your story is selected for inclusion, we will be happy to include a link to your website, social media or other online project.

If you have a *Wordpress* blog and would like to distribute this book and my other books too, you can do so very easily with our free plugin. Get the plugin by going to your Wordpress dashboard and selecting *Plugins/Add New* from the menu. Then type 'free books section' into the search box. The plugin allows you to offer good quality free content for your visitors and also enables you to earn Amazon affiliate commissions at the same time.

White Dove Books

Copyright © 2006 - 2018 White Dove Books

All Rights Reserved

Made in the USA
Middletown, DE
21 May 2020